ANIMALS

Iain MacLeod-Brudenell
Photographs by Zul Mukhida

Contents

A&C Black · London

About this book

What's your favourite animal? Perhaps it's your pet or maybe it's a wild animal that you've seen only in books or on television. This book is about real and imaginary animals. It shows you how to make craft objects based on animals and gives you plenty of ideas to help you design your own craft objects.

This book will tell you about stories, traditions and crafts from around the world which are based on animals. Try to find out more about these animals and crafts. You will find information about places to visit and books to read at the back of the book.

Some of the craft activities in this book are more complicated than others and will take longer to finish. It might be fun to ask some friends to help with these activities, such as making the lion mask on page 6.

Before you start working on any of the craft projects, read through the instructions carefully. Each step-by-step instruction has a number. Look for the same number in the picture to see what each stage of your model should look like.

Before you begin

Collect together everything listed in the 'you will need box'.

Ask an adult's permission if you are going to use a sharp tool, dye cloth or use an oven.

Prepare a clear work surface.

If the activity is going to be messy, cover the surface with old newspaper or a waterproof sheet.

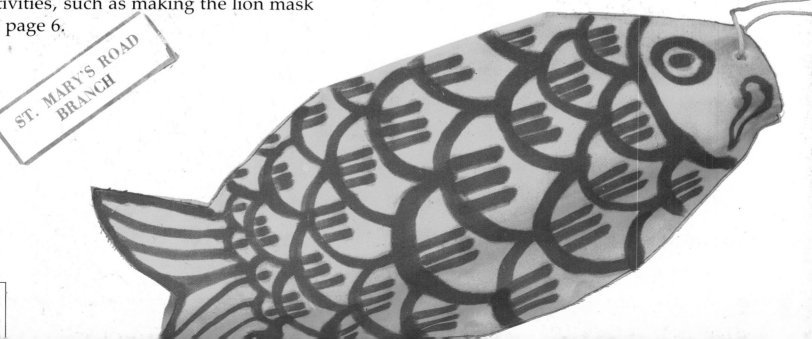

3

Animal people

In many stories, animals are main characters. They are given human qualities, such as being honest or greedy. In Aesop's fables, talking animals are used to show human faults. Do you think that animals and people have similar characteristics?

'Puss in Boots' is the story of a very clever cat, who wears long boots. After many adventures Puss in Boots makes his master rich and powerful. Today, this story is often retold in pantomime.

Try making a glove puppet of Puss in Boots

> You will need: felt, glue, self-hardening clay or salt dough (see page 30), a pin, paints and paint brushes, a large needle and thread, scissors, braid or scraps of material.

1 Cut out a tunic shape from felt. The tunic must be big enough for your hand to fit inside. Glue or sew the side seams of the tunic together. Decorate with braid or scraps of material.

2 Cut out two rectangles of felt for the legs. On each rectangle, glue or sew the long edges together. Glue or stitch the legs to the wrong side of the front of the tunic.

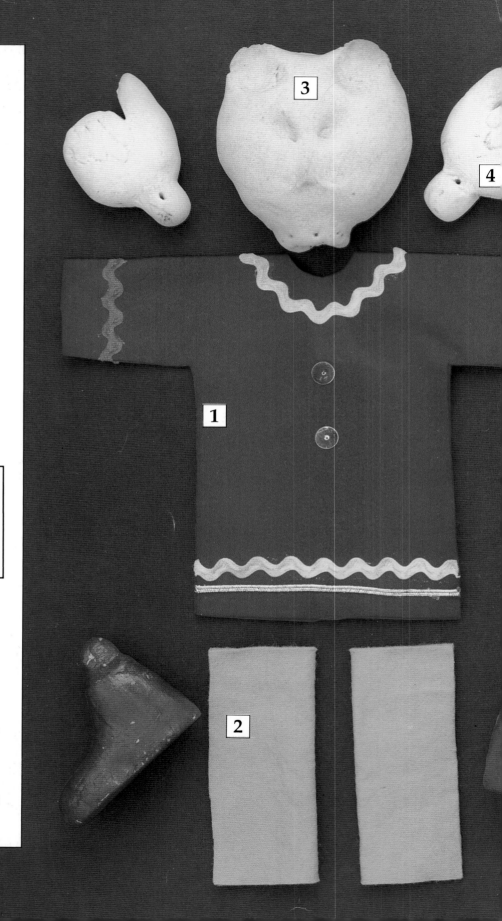

3 Make the head from a ball of clay or salt dough. Make the head hollow. Squeeze the bottom of the head into a neck, which will fit into the neck of the tunic.

Make about eight holes around the edge of the neck of the head with a pin. The holes should be big enough for a large needle and thread to pass through. Leave the clay to dry or bake the salt dough and then paint the head.

4 Make two paws and two boots from the clay or dough. Pinch the ends as shown. Make one hole which runs through each end. Then make another hole, so that the holes are at quarter turns. Leave the clay to dry or bake the dough. Then paint the paws and boots.

5 To join the head to the tunic, stitch through the neck of the tunic and then through a hole in the puppet's neck. Continue until you have stitched all the way round. Stitch the boots to the legs and then stitch the paws to the arms of the tunic in the same way.

Put your glove puppet on your hand and make Puss in Boots move. Try to make puppets of other animal characters and put on a puppet show.

5

Lion tales

In Nigeria a lion is thought of as proud and lazy, but in many European countries a lion is thought of as brave.

Try making a lion mask

You will need: cardboard, masking tape or a stapler, newspaper torn into strips, wallpaper paste without fungicide, scraps of paper and material for decoration, scissors, egg boxes, paints and paint brushes, felt and glue.

1 Cut the cardboard into long strips which are about 5cm wide. You can use the card from an old flattened box. Make a hoop which is big enough to go over your head and rest on your shoulders. Fasten the cardboard strip into a hoop with tape or a stapler.

Use the hoop as the base for a cardboard cage. Fasten a number of strips, which fit over your head, from side to side of the base, as shown.

Cover the cage with a layer of strips of torn newspaper which have been dipped into wallpaper paste. When the cage is covered with papier-mâché, leave it to dry. Then paste another layer on top. Cover with about four layers of papier-mâché. Leave to dry.

2 Put the cage over your head and feel where you should make the holes for the lion's eyes and nostrils. Take the mask off and cut out the eye and nostril holes. Make the lion's features with crumpled paper and egg boxes, and glue on to the mask. Cover the mask with another layer of papier-mâché. Leave to dry.

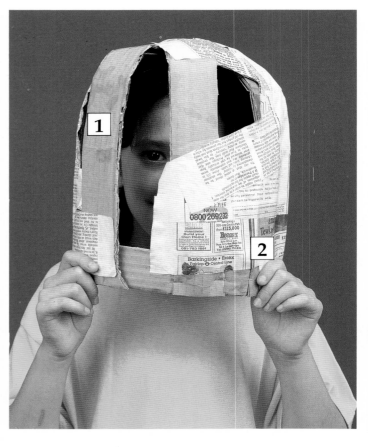

3 Paint the mask. You can use coloured felt to make a mane.

Mythical creatures

Hundreds of years ago, sailors were often the only people to travel great distances. On their return home, they told stories of strange and wonderful creatures that they had seen. Artists listened to the sailors' descriptions and made drawings of the creatures. Sometimes the drawings were accurate but sometimes the creatures looked magical and amazing.

Many creatures and monsters in legends and myths are a combination of two animals or part of an animal and part of a person. A centaur is a mythical creature which is half-horse and half-man. A mermaid is a creature which is half-woman and half-fish. The griffin is a monster which is a combination of two animals. An ancient story says that the griffin is the offspring of a lion and an eagle. The griffin kept guard over hidden treasures.

Try making your own paper creatures which are a mixture of animal parts or a mixture of animals and people.

> **You will need: a pencil, scissors, coloured cardboard, paper fasteners, a knitting needle or hole punch, lolly sticks, glue.**

Before you start, it might help to look at photographs of different kinds of animals, such as wild and farm animals. Look at the shapes of their heads, legs, arms, paws, beaks and wings.

1 Choose one animal and on coloured cardboard draw the outline of its head, its body, its arms and legs separately. Cut them out carefully.

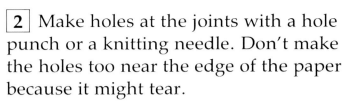

2 Make holes at the joints with a hole punch or a knitting needle. Don't make the holes too near the edge of the paper because it might tear.

3 Use paper fasteners to join the parts together.

4 Make parts for lots of different kinds of animals. How many creatures can you make? Try making a mermaid or a centaur. Where will your creature live?

To make a creature into a shadow puppet, glue or tape sticks to the back of the head and the elbows or wrists. Let the legs dangle. Stand in front of a well-lit wall, move the sticks and see the shadow of the creature move.

9

Dragon fire

According to legends, dragons lived in many parts of the world. In Japanese and Chinese legends, dragons are friendly and help to keep order. But in European legends, they are often cruel and cunning.

Look out for dragons on flags and statues.

Try making a flying dragon

You will need: coloured paper or thin card, scissors, a pencil, a hole punch or knitting needle, two paper fasteners, a 26cm length of thin dowel, three lengths of coated garden wire about 45cm each.

1 To help you draw the dragon's shape, look at pictures of dragons in books. Draw and cut out a paper dragon's body with a head and tail.

2 Draw and cut out four separate legs. Use a hole punch or knitting needle to make two holes in each leg – one at the foot and the other near the top as shown.

3 Make one hole in the back of the body for the back legs and one hole at the front of the body for the front legs.

4 Join two legs to the front of the body with a paper fastener as shown. Then join the two back legs to the body in the same way.

5 Draw and cut out two wings. Make a hole near the outer tip of each wing as shown. Make tabs by folding back 1cm of paper at the base of the wings.

6 Take one wing and glue or tape the tab to the body. Attach the other wing to the other side of the dragon's body in the same way.

7 Make holes for the stick in the body – one near the top in the middle and the other at the bottom in the middle.

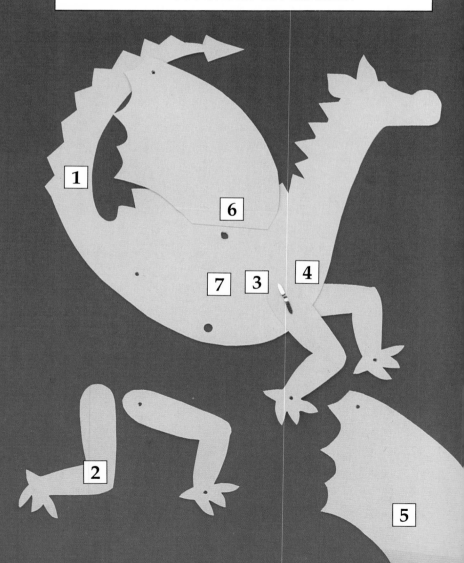

8 Join the stick to the body by pushing it through the holes you have just made in the body. You may need to use a dab of glue or some tape as well.

9 Place the middle of one length of wire at the base of the stick. Wrap the wire round the stick twice.

10 Thread one end of the wire through the hole in one of the wings. Twist the end of the wire to make it secure. Join the other end of the wire to the other wing in the same way.

11 Wrap the second length of wire round the stick as before. Join one end of the wire to one of the front legs and the other end to one of the back legs.

12 Wrap the third length of wire round the stick as before. Join one end to one back leg and the other end to one front leg as you did before.

Decorate your dragon with paper shapes. To make your dragon fly, push the wire up and down the stick.

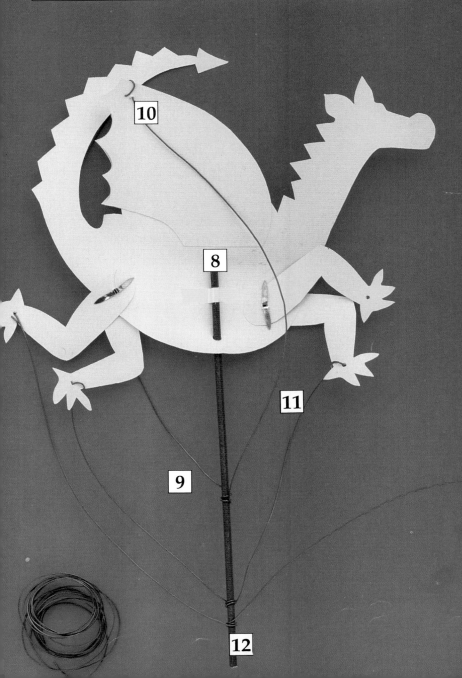

The ocean deep

'Mother of pearl' buttons are made from sea shells. Usually, the buttons are uneven at the back and may even have shell markings. They are pearly white and shimmer. In the east end of London, some costermongers, people who sell fruit and vegetables from barrows, sew thousands of pearl buttons on to dark suits, which they wear on special occasions.

In the nineteenth century the Trimshian, Kwakiutl and Tlingit people of Canada decorated blankets with pearl buttons. Often the designs on the blankets were in the shape of killer whales or other sea creatures. Similar blankets are still made today.

Try making a button blanket

> You will need: felt, plastic pearly buttons, sequins, latex glue, a needle and thread.

Draw your creature on felt and cut it out. It's best to use a bold coloured felt, such as black, red, yellow or blue. Glue or sew the animal shape on to a different coloured piece of felt or fabric.

First, sew buttons or sequins on to the outline of the creature. Then sew buttons or sequins on for features, such as eyes. If your animal is a fish, add fins and a back bone. You can cover the creature's shape with buttons or sequins or leave it plain, whichever you think looks best. Try to make a border from buttons to frame your picture.

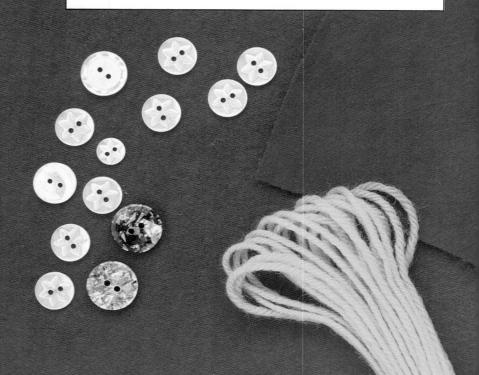

Try making your button blanket into a
wall hanging or a cushion.

13

Flying fish

In Japan, on May 5th, it's Children's Day, which is a national holiday. Many children hang kites in the shape of carp outside. The kites can be made from paper or fabric. When the wind blows, the carp kites fill with air and look as if they are swimming in water. The carp stands for strength, energy and long life.

Try making a carp kite to fly in the wind

You will need: paper or fabric, scissors, glue or a needle and thread and four sewing pins, a strip of cardboard, a hole punch, a bamboo stick, string, felt tips or fabric markers.

1 Fold a piece of paper or fabric into a rectangle and draw the outline of a fish with a wide mouth. Glue the four corners of the paper together or pin the four edges of the fabric together. Cut out the shape of the fish.

2 Join the sides of the fish together with glue or close stitches. Leave both ends free for the wind to blow through.

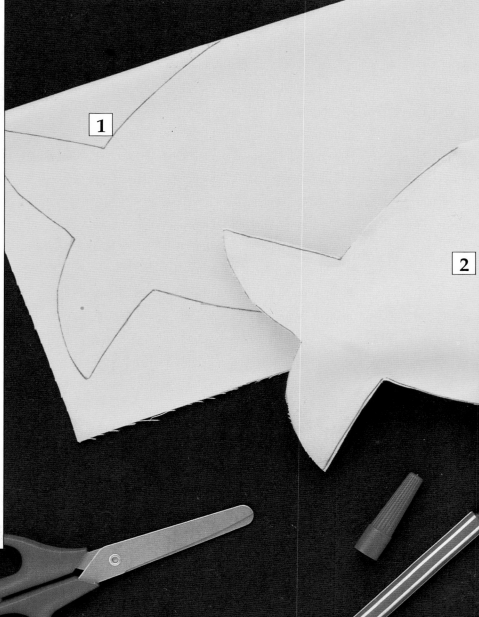

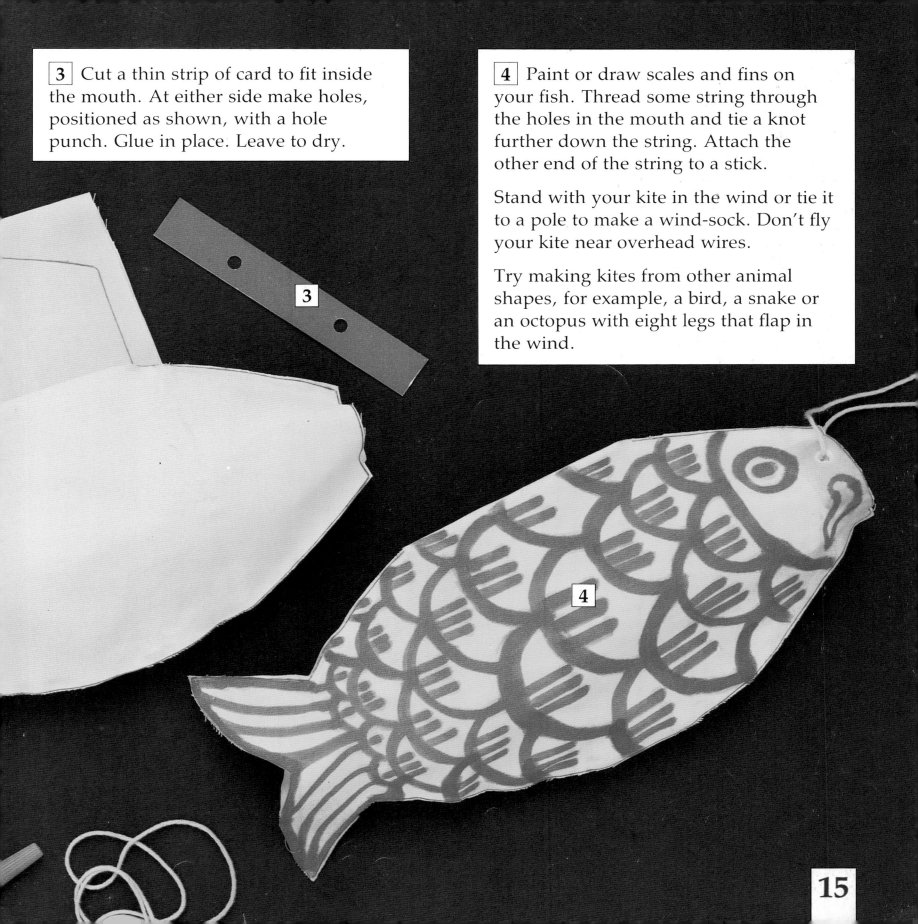

3 Cut a thin strip of card to fit inside the mouth. At either side make holes, positioned as shown, with a hole punch. Glue in place. Leave to dry.

4 Paint or draw scales and fins on your fish. Thread some string through the holes in the mouth and tie a knot further down the string. Attach the other end of the string to a stick.

Stand with your kite in the wind or tie it to a pole to make a wind-sock. Don't fly your kite near overhead wires.

Try making kites from other animal shapes, for example, a bird, a snake or an octopus with eight legs that flap in the wind.

15

Noah and Jonah

In many parts of the world, there are stories about a great flood. Here is one from the Bible. God warned a man called Noah of the coming flood, so Noah built a huge boat called an ark for his family and two of each kind of animal. After forty days and forty nights the flood stopped and all the animals were set free. Then the first rainbow appeared, which was God's promise to Noah that the world would never be destroyed again.

This painted silk picture shows a Moslem version of the story of the flood.

The story of Jonah and the whale also appears in the Bible. It tells of Jonah who lived in the belly of a whale for three days. Find out more about this story.

A thaumatrope is a Victorian spinning toy, which appears to make pictures combine. A thaumatrope which has a picture of a goldfish on one side and a picture of a bowl on the other spins to show a goldfish in a bowl. Try making some thaumatropes which put the animals inside the ark or Jonah inside the whale.

> **You will need: cardboard, a pair of compasses or an old yoghurt pot, a knitting needle, string, a pencil, scissors, paints and paint brushes or scraps of paper and coloured pens.**

1 Draw two circles the same size on to cardboard. You can make the circles with a compass or by drawing round the top of a yoghurt pot. Cut them out.

2 Decide which story you want to show, then paint, draw or make a paper collage of two pictures which tell the story.

3 Stick the circles together. Make two holes 5 mm from the edge of the circle as shown. Thread a length of string through each hole and tightly knot it at the ends.

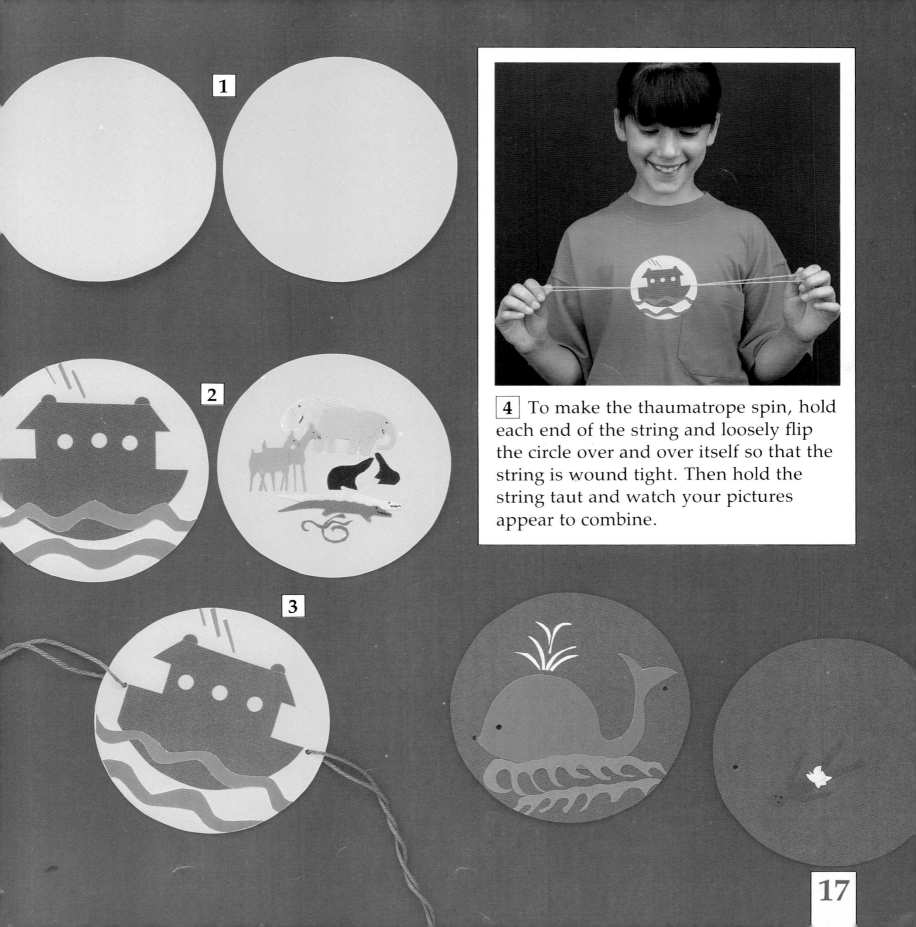

1

2

3

4 To make the thaumatrope spin, hold each end of the string and loosely flip the circle over and over itself so that the string is wound tight. Then hold the string taut and watch your pictures appear to combine.

17

The Haida Raven

The Haida people from North America tell the story of a raven who escaped from a great flood, by perching on the top of the highest mountain. As the flood ebbed, the Raven felt hungry and ate thousands of shellfish. Then he rested after his large meal. Suddenly he noticed a giant clam shell, full of tiny creatures, but the Raven was too full to eat them.

The Raven sang sweetly to the creatures and told them stories of a beautiful world full of wonderful animals. Slowly, one by one, the creatures climbed from the shell. The Raven looked after them, taught them how to hunt and fish, build canoes and play tricks. Soon the creatures were clever and didn't need the Raven to look after them any more. The creatures were people.

The pictures on Haida paintings and carvings are similar to jigsaws because they are made from separate shapes which fit together to make one picture. Certain shapes are used to show different parts of the body.

Copy these basic Haida shapes on to cardboard, cut them out and make them into a picture. Your finished picture will look very bold if you colour the shapes with only three colours.

Try inventing your own jigsaw shapes. You can use them as templates to trace around and design your own patterns and pictures. Try decorating a t-shirt with your patterns. **Before you begin, ask an adult and read the instructions on the fabric paint carefully.**

19

Origami cygnets

Origami is the Japanese art of paper folding. Try making an origami cygnet, which is a baby swan. Origami can take some practice so if you don't get it right first time, try again.

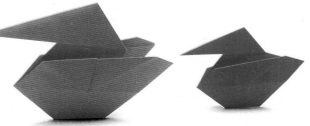

You will need: origami paper or squares of coloured flimsy paper, approximately 17.5cm square.

1 Fold the paper towards you diagonally.

2 Turn over the paper so it's coloured-side down.

3 Fold the top corner to meet the diagonal fold.

4 Then fold the bottom corner to meet the diagonal fold.

5 Fold the white point to the left.

Fold the paper to the left along the dotted line.

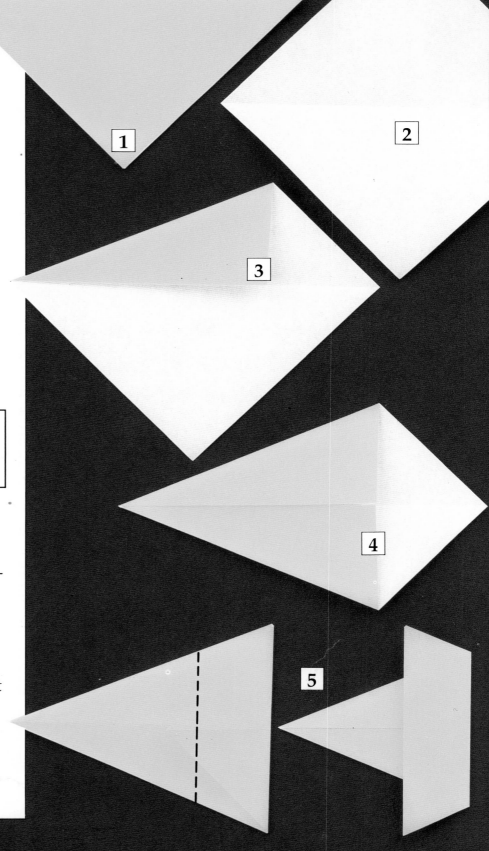

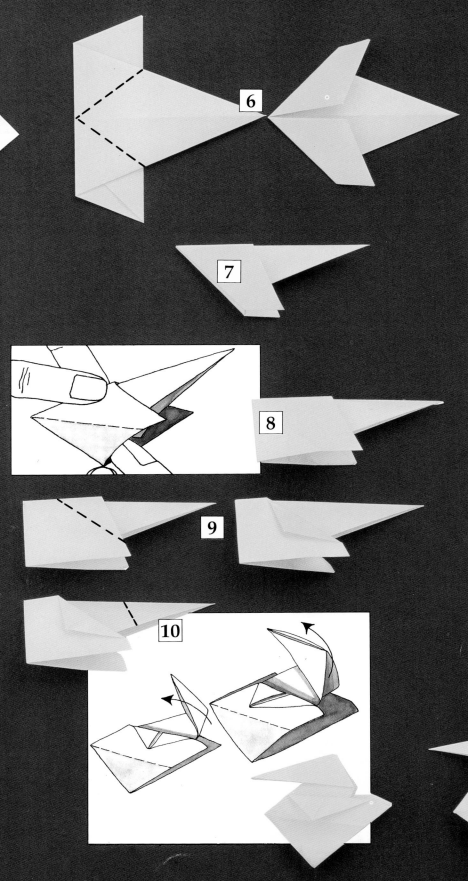

6 Turn over the paper so the point faces right.

Fold along each dotted line into the middle crease.

7 Fold the shape in half along the middle crease.

8 Pinch the top of the two wings on the middle crease and pull out the triangle of paper from underneath.

9 Make one wing tip by folding down the dotted line. Repeat on the other side to make the other wing tip.

10 Make a crease on the dotted line for the head.

To make the head, open out the point and fold the crease backwards to the left.

11 To make a base for the cygnet to rest on, fold up a small triangle at the bottom.

Open out the shape along the bottom fold and press the small triangle inwards.

21

Paper-cut peacocks

In China, paper-cutting is a traditional craft. Coloured paper is cut into intricate patterns with scissors that are razor-sharp. The patterns are used to make pictures. Often the paper-cut pictures are mounted on to boldly coloured paper so that the complicated paper cutting stands out.

Here are a few suggestions for cutting different patterns from paper which can be used to make a peacock. Try to invent your own ways of cutting paper as well.

> **You will need: coloured paper, scissors, a pencil, glue.**

[1] Cut out the shapes for the body, legs and the head feathers.

[2] To make tail feathers, fold a strip of paper in half lengthways and cut triangles from the centre fold.

3 To make the 'eye' parts of the tail feathers, fold a square of paper into four and cut out a quarter circle. Experiment with cutting small shapes on the folds.

4 You can make other decorations for the peacock's body by cutting three oval shapes which fit inside each other. Fold one oval in half and cut small triangles around the edges and along the centre fold. Glue the ovals on top of each other as shown.

Try creating your own animals from paper cuts. Remember, it's best to cut on the fold. If you want to make your pattern more complicated, re-fold the paper and cut some more shapes on a different fold.

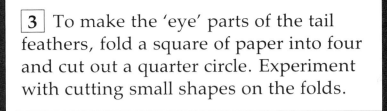

3

4

Snakes and serpents

There are stories about snakes and serpents from all over the world. In an ancient Greek story, a monster called Medusa had snakes instead of hair. Her face was so terrible that anyone who looked at her turned to stone. Eventually, a hero called Perseus cut off her head by using a mirror as a shield. He looked only at her reflection, and not at her face.

Here is an Aztec legend about a serpent. The Aztec gods told the Aztec people that they should settle only in the place where they found an eagle with a snake hanging from its beak. When the people saw an eagle in the middle of a lake, perched on a cactus with a snake in its beak, they built their city called Tenochtitlan. This is the same site on which Mexico City stands today.

Try making a zig-zag snake

You will need: two toothpaste boxes which are the same size, coloured paper and glue or thick emulsion paints and paint brushes, scissors.

1 Cover one toothpaste box with coloured paper or paint it with emulsion paint. If you cover it with paper, paste all over the paper first. Cover the other box with a different coloured paper or paint. Cut the ends from both boxes. Flatten each box and cut into strips which are about 1cm wide.

1

2 Fold one strip in half and poke its ends through the opened-out ends of a second different coloured strip as shown.

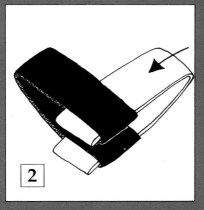

3 To make a zig-zag, poke the third strip through the ends of the second strip. Continue joining the strips together until you have used all the strips.

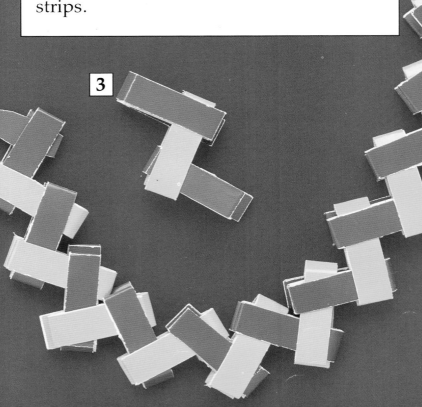

4 Cut out a cardboard head and glue it to one end of the snake. Make a tail for the other end.

What other animals can you make in this way?

Try making your snake into a puppet. Attach sticks along the back of the snake. Move them to make the snake wriggle.

Lucky animals

Many animals are thought to bring good luck. In ancient Rome, in the middle of the night, a flock of geese heard the Gauls preparing to make a surprise attack. The geese made so much noise they woke the Romans up in time to defend their city. The geese became known as 'watch dogs'.

In parts of Pakistan, floors are decorated with lucky animal patterns, called Sathia, made from dots of coloured powder. Often, Sathia in the shape of lucky fish and horseshoes decorate the doorsteps of people who are about to get married.

Try making a Sathia decoration

You will need: an old shoe box lid, coloured powder paint, a bodkin or knitting needle, a cork tile or old piece of carpet, paper, a felt pen.

1 Draw your lucky animal on to the upturned box lid. Put the box lid on to a cork tile or old piece of carpet. Make holes with the bodkin or knitting needle along the drawn outline, but do not make the holes too close together.

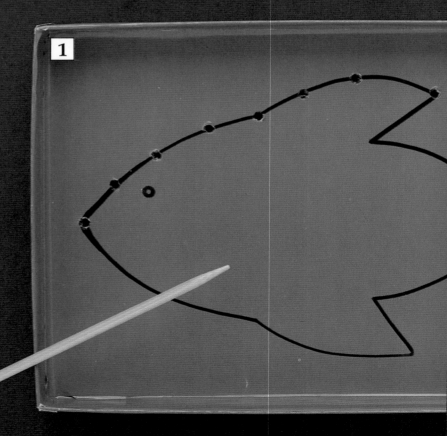

2 Put your box lid on to some clean dry concrete outside – **remember to ask for permission first** – or on to some paper. Use a spoon to sprinkle powder into the tray over the design. Lift the tray slightly and tap it gently at the sides. Powder should fall through the holes in the shape of your animal. If it doesn't, try again, making the holes slightly bigger.

In Tamil Nadu, South India, at the entrance to some villages, there are huge models of horses made from clay. The horses are thought to bring good luck and protect the village from harm.

Try making your own model horse from papier-mâché

You will need: six cardboard tubes which have the same diameter and one which is slightly bigger, masking tape, newspaper torn into strips, a small bowl of wallpaper paste without fungicide, paints and paint brushes, scissors, felt.

1 Cut the six tubes to make lengths for four legs, a neck and head. Take one of the leg-tubes, slightly flatten it and cut the top at an angle so that it fits the body-tube. Cut the other leg-tubes in this way. Cut the top and bottom of the neck-tube and the top of the head tube at an angle as well.

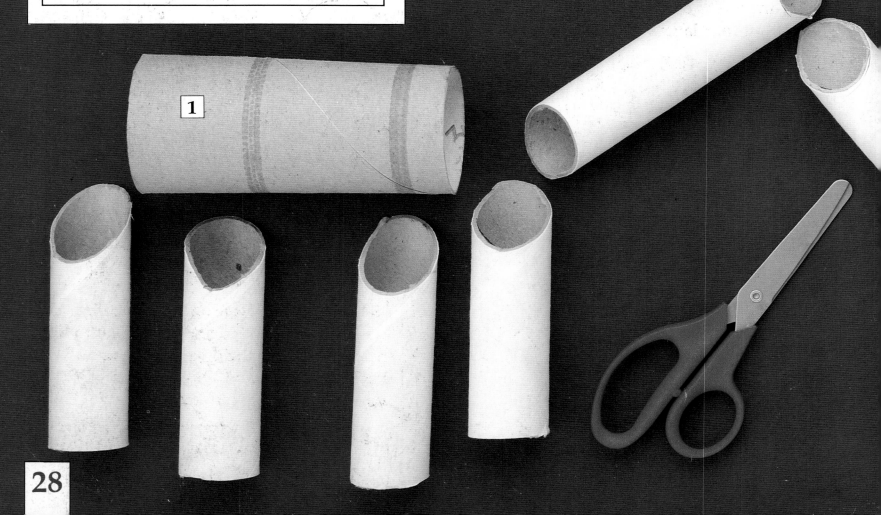

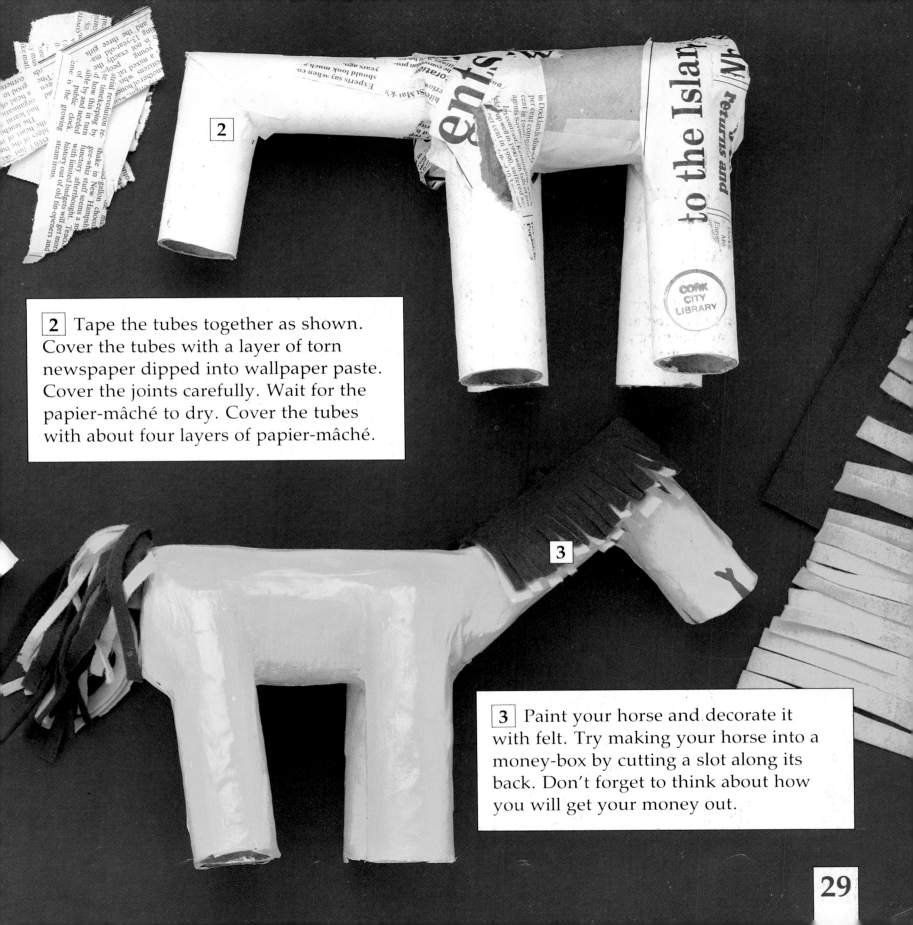

2 Tape the tubes together as shown. Cover the tubes with a layer of torn newspaper dipped into wallpaper paste. Cover the joints carefully. Wait for the papier-mâché to dry. Cover the tubes with about four layers of papier-mâché.

3 Paint your horse and decorate it with felt. Try making your horse into a money-box by cutting a slot along its back. Don't forget to think about how you will get your money out.

29

More things to think about

This book shows you how to make and model salt dough and papier-mâché, cut and fold paper and sew clothes for a puppet. You can use these different craft techniques to make your own objects based on animals.

To get ideas for making your own craft objects, think about some of the different kinds of animals in the world and the stories you know about them. Visit your local art gallery, museum or crafts centre to see how artists have shown animals now and in the past. Look out for animals on pictures, statues and signs in your town or village.

Do you believe that dragons and unicorns existed long ago? There are many stories about imaginary animals in fairy tales and ancient myths. Read some fairy tales or myths and try making a craft version of an imaginary animal.

Every country has its own customs and traditions, and some are based on animals. During Chinese New Year celebrations, people dress in large dragon costumes and dance in processions in the streets. Choose a country, such as Japan, China, India or France and see if you can find some traditional stories or celebrations which include animals. You could use these ideas for your own craft projects on animals.

Think about what animals look like in real life, and where different types of animals live: in water, on land or in the air. Do you have a pet cat, dog or fish at home? Try sketching your pet. You can look at photographs of wild animals in books and magazines, or watch nature programmes on television. Look at the shape of the animal's head, body and legs.

Does it swim, crawl, slither or run? Keep a notebook of your findings and sketches of the animals you draw. These will be helpful when you come to make your craft object.

Before you make your craft object, think about the best craft technique to use, for example you could model salt dough or papier-mâché, or cut and fold paper. Do you want the finished model to be flat or three-dimensional? Will it have moving parts? Do you want to wear it as a mask or will it hang from the ceiling? When you have answered these and other questions, think carefully about the best way of making your model and the best materials to use.

Experiment with different kinds of decoration for your craft object. You can give it spots, stripes, feathers, fur or scales. Think about all the different ways you can create these textures with paper, cloth or by modelling salt dough or papier-mâché. Try making a tiny lion puppet for your finger or a giant jigsaw paper-cut based on Haida shapes.

How to make salt dough

You will need: 325g plain flour, 225g salt, 250ml water, 1 tablespoon of oil, a wooden spoon, a bowl, a baking tray, greaseproof paper, an oven set to Gas Mark 2 (300F or 150C).

Mix the dry ingredients together. Then add the water and oil. Shake some flour over your hands and knead the mixture into a dough.

When you have modelled the dough into the shape you want, put it on to a baking tray lined with greaseproof paper. **Ask an adult to help you put it in the oven.** Bake for about one and a quarter hours, until the model is hard.

How to find out more

Information books about animals

* 24 hours Barrie Watts (Franklin Watts)
A series of books which takes an hour by hour look at the lives of animals and plants in different habitats.

* Handmade habitats Paul Wright (A&C Black)
How to create wildlife habitats on a small scale.

* Stopwatch (A&C Black)
The life cycle of a minibeast, with full colour photographs – a helpful reference for preliminary craft sketches.

Fiction

And pigs might fly Michael Morpurgo
(A&C Black)

Charlotte's Web E. B. White (Puffin)

The Orchard Book of Greek Myths Retold by Geraldine McCaughrean (Orchard)

The Orchard Book of Fairy Tales Retold by Rose Impey (Orchard)

The Orchard Book of Poems compiled by Adrian Mitchell (Orchard)

Books about crafts and technology

* Fresh start (Franklin Watts)
A step-by-step approach to different craft media. Titles include **Clay**, **Fabric art**, **Papier mâché**, **Masks**, **Paper crafts** and **Jewellery crafts**.

* Arts and crafts (Wayland)
A clear step-by-step approach to crafts with ideas for developing designs. Titles include **Batik and tie-dye**, **Block printing** and **Weaving**.

* Toybox science Chris Ollerenshaw and Pat Triggs (A&C Black)
Scientific principles explained through toys. A helpful guide to making working models.

* Make it work Peter Firmin (A&C Black)
How to build working models from rubbish, including the technology of pulleys, levers and winches.

* indicates a series rather than one book.

Places to visit

The following list gives a selection of places to visit which have major collections of objects from around the world. Don't forget to look in your local town or city museum too.

Commonwealth Institute
230 Kensington High Street, London W8
Each country in the commonwealth has its own display of art and crafts.

Horniman Museum
100 London Road, London SE23
A collection showing arts, crafts and religions of the world.

Pitt Rivers Museum
South Parks Road, Oxford OX1 3PP
Lieutenant General Pitt Rivers, born in 1827, collected a wide range of objects from countries all over the world which he visited as a soldier.

Victoria and Albert Museum
Cromwell Road, London SW7
A vast collection of nineteenth century artefacts.

Useful addresses

World-Wide Fund for Nature (WWF UK)
Panda House, Weyside Park, Godalming, Surrey GU7 1XR

WATCH, The Green, Witham Park, Waterside South, Lincoln LN5 7JR
An environmental club for young people.

Index

First published 1993
A & C Black (Publishers) Limited
35 Bedford Row, London WC1R 4JH

ISBN 0 7136 3712 9
© 1993 A & C Black (Publishers)
Limited

A CIP catalogue record for this book
is available from the British Library.

Acknowledgements
Line drawings by Barbara Pegg
Photographs by Zul Mukhida, except
for: p14, p16 Life File Photographic
Agency.

With grateful thanks to Langford and
Hill Limited, London, for supplying
all art materials.

Craft objects made by Dorothy Moir
except for those on p4–5, p6–7, p8–9,
p28–29 which were made by Tracy
Brunt.

Filmset by Rowland Phototypesetting
Limited, Bury St Edmunds, Suffolk
Printed in England by Cambus Litho